ANGELS

INTRODUCTION

ANGELS

Greetings Beloved ,

I am writting this book to teach and guide you concerning God's angels. We are living in the last days and this information and divine knowledge is essential in a believer's life.

We live in a spiritual world that is physical at the same time. Inorder for you to succeed in this world you need to be equipped both spiritually and physically. I hope you enjoy your read and by the end of this book you are empowered and revived!

Chapter 1

The Spiritual World.

The spiritual world is very real, though it is unseen by the physical eye. When we are born into the earth realm we first see with our physical eyes. It is by God's special grace that the spiritual scales are removed of our spiritual eyes.

ANGELS

We live in world that is made up of the both the physical and the spiritual .When God first created the world ,He created it in the spiritual realm and when He spoke the words of creation they manifested in the physical world .

Everything that is tangible in the physical realm or earthly realm first started in the spiritual realm .We are spiritual beings who live in a physical body.Unfortunately because of sin ,we were separated from God and slowly our spiritual nature died as well.

The further you move away from God ,the more you die spiritually.This is why most people are unable to see in the spiritual realm on a daily basis or ,to grasp the spiritual things or to enjoy the spiritual realm.God designed us with the ability to see physically and spiritually ,this is His desire for us to be able to function in both worlds.

You do not have to be a prophet or a man or woman of God inorder to see in the spiritual realm or to participate in it.Everyone has this ability ,the key is in having your spirit activated and eyes open by a God given Spiritual Parent or Parents.

They carry the key that can unlock you and birth you into the divine understanding of the spiritual realm and spiritual life.The spiritual life should be your second nature as a believer.So many things can be received ,unlocked or avoided ,if your spiritual eyes and ears are functioning.

Many people could have avoided being in car accidents , involved in painful marriages, involved in bad relationships, avoided terrible situations at work ,in school etc if they had their eyes and ears spiritually opened.

2 Corinthians 4:18

18 So we don't look at the troubles we can see now; rather, we fix our gaze on things that cannot be seen. For the things we see now will soon be gone, but the things we cannot see will last forever.

Genesis 1 1:27

The Account of Creation

1 In the beginning God created the heavens and the earth.[a] 2 The earth was formless and empty, and darkness covered the deep waters. And the Spirit of God was hovering over the surface of the waters.

3 Then God said, "Let there be light," and there was light. 4 And God saw that the light was good. Then he separated the light from the darkness. 5 God called the light "day" and the darkness "night."

And evening passed and morning came, marking the first day.

6 Then God said, "Let there be a space between the waters, to separate the waters of the heavens from the waters of the earth." 7 And that is what happened. God made this space to separate the

waters of the earth from the waters of the heavens. 8 God called the space "sky."

And evening passed and morning came, marking the second day.

9 Then God said, "Let the waters beneath the sky flow together into one place, so dry ground may appear." And that is what happened. 10 God called the dry ground "land" and the waters "seas." And God saw that it was good. 11 Then God said, "Let the land sprout with vegetation—every sort of seed-bearing plant, and trees that grow seed-bearing fruit. These seeds will then produce the kinds of plants and trees from which they came." And that is what happened. 12 The land produced vegetation—all sorts of seed-bearing plants, and trees with seed-bearing fruit. Their seeds produced plants and trees of the same kind. And God saw that it was good.

13 And evening passed and morning came, marking

the third day.

14 Then God said, "Let lights appear in the sky to separate the day from the night. Let them be signs to mark the seasons, days, and years. 15 Let these lights in the sky shine down on the earth." And that is what happened. 16 God made two great lights—the larger one to govern the day, and the smaller one to govern the night. He also made the stars. 17 God set these lights in the sky to light the earth, 18 to govern the day and night, and to separate the light from the darkness. And God saw that it was good.

19 And evening passed and morning came, marking the fourth day.

20 Then God said, "Let the waters swarm with fish and other life. Let the skies be filled with birds of every kind." 21 So God created great sea creatures and every living thing that scurries and swarms in

the water, and every sort of bird—each producing offspring of the same kind. And God saw that it was good. 22 Then God blessed them, saying, "Be fruitful and multiply. Let the fish fill the seas, and let the birds multiply on the earth."

23 And evening passed and morning came, marking the fifth day.

24 Then God said, "Let the earth produce every sort of animal, each producing offspring of the same kind—livestock, small animals that scurry along the ground, and wild animals." And that is what happened. 25 God made all sorts of wild animals, livestock, and small animals, each able to produce offspring of the same kind. And God saw that it was good.

26 Then God said, "Let us make human beings[b] in our image, to be like us. They will reign over the fish in the sea, the birds in the sky, the livestock, all the

wild animals on the earth,[c] and the small animals that scurry along the ground."

27 So God created human beings[d] in his own image.

   In the image of God he created them;

   male and female he createdl

When God created the heavens and the earth, He created both spiritual beings and living beings. He created the human race and the angelic beings. In this book I will be focusing on the angelic beings.

I am very excited for you to learn more about the hidden mysteries of God's kingdom and his creation.

1 Corinthians 2:9

but just as it is written, "THINGS WHICH EYE HAS NOT SEEN AND EAR HAS NOT HEARD, AND which HAVE NOT ENTERED THE HEART OF MAN, ALL THAT GOD HAS PREPARED FOR THOSE WHO LOVE HIM."

1 Corinthians 2:10

For to us God revealed them through the Spirit; for the Spirit searches all things, even the depths of God.

Ephesians 1:9

He made known to us the mystery of His will, according to His kind intention which He purposed in Him

Colossians 1:26

that is, the mystery which has been hidden from the

past ages and generations, but has now been manifested to His saints,

Jeremiah 33:3

Call to Me and I will answer you, and I will tell you great and mighty things, which you do not know.'

CHAPTER 2

Life In God's Kingdom

The spiritual world is not a realm only meant for the prophets of God or anointed men and women of God. Everyone is entitled to see and to participate in spiritual world after being born again. When you receive the Lord Jesus Christ as your Lord and personal Saviour, you have entered through a door of salvation and into his divine kingdom.

The Lord Jesus Christ mentions in the verse below that he is a spiritual door. When you become born again you gain access to possessing everything that comes with the heavenly kingdom of God.

John 10:9-10

9 I am the door. If anyone enters by me, he will be saved and will go in and out and find pasture. 10 The thief comes only to steal and kill and destroy. I came that they may have life and have it abundantly.

The spiritual world exists and it is much more real than the physical world. It also has spiritual creatures that exist and live in it. They are godly spiritual beings and evil spiritual beings.

The godly spiritual beings are on God's side and are

working for God and work according to his will. The spiritual beings are messengers of God and have been created to help God run the world and the rest of his other creation. Every thing the godly spiritual beings do or say is mandated by God .

Unfortunately in the spiritual world they are also evil spiritual beings ,just as it is in the physical world ,we have good and evil people. The spiritual world is no different ,as a matter of fact ,every thing that manifests or exists in the physical world first happens in the spiritual world.

If you see great things happening in your life that means spiritually all is well for you and God is with you. When things begin to go bad. This is an indication that the enemy is around and he is tempering around with your life.

The spiritual world is very real even though it is invisible to those who have their spiritual eyes closed. The angels and demons in this world are very real and very active.

There is a constant warfare going on in the spiritual realm between God's angels and the devil and his evil kingdom.

This is a warfare of the safety and salvation of humanity and God is in the business of redeeming his people.

Jude 6

6 And the angels who did not keep their positions of authority but abandoned their proper dwelling—these he has kept in darkness, bound with everlasting chains for judgment on the great Day.

Angels were created and are assigned daily to protect us. The Lord Jesus Christ came and defeated the enemy and his evil plans against us, but there is still an on going fight of our faith until the Lord returns again for the second time.

ANGELS

So you also must be ready, because the Son of Man will come at an hour when you do not expect him.

Matthew 24:44

And let us consider how we may spur one another on toward love and good deeds, not giving up meeting together, as some are in the habit of doing, but encouraging one another—and all the more as you see the Day approaching.

Hebrews 10:24-25

He who testifies to these things says, "Yes, I am

coming soon."

Amen. Come, Lord Jesus.

Revelation 22:20

Therefore keep watch, because you do not know on what day your Lord will come.

Matthew 24:42

The end of all things is near. Therefore be alert and

of sober mind so that you may pray.

1 Peter 4:7

"Look, I am coming soon! My reward is with me, and I will give to each person according to what they have done."

Revelation 22:12

"I am the Alpha and the Omega," says the Lord God, "who is, and who was, and who is to come, the Almighty."

Revelation 1:8

ANGELS

And now, dear children, continue in him, so that when he appears we may be confident and unashamed before him at his coming.

1 John 2:28

They were looking intently up into the sky as he was going, when suddenly two men dressed in white stood beside them. "Men of Galilee," they said, "why do you stand here looking into the sky? This same Jesus, who has been taken from you into heaven, will come back in the same way you have seen him go into heaven."

Acts 1:10-11

But do not forget this one thing, dear friends: With the Lord a day is like a thousand years, and a thousand years are like a day.

2 Peter 3:8

I am coming soon. Hold on to what you have, so that no one will take your crown.

Revelation 3:11

Being confident of this, that he who began a good work in you will carry it on to completion until the day of Christ Jesus.

Philippians 1:6

And do not grieve the Holy Spirit of God, with whom you were sealed for the day of redemption.

In this book I want to focus on God's angels even though the spiritual is very broad and there is so much more to reveal.

Chapter 3.

GOD'S ANGELS.

Hebrews 1:14

14 Therefore, angels are only servants—spirits sent to care for people who will inherit salvation.

Before God created the earth ,He created the heavens which is part of the spiritual world and after he created it ,He created the angelic beings who live in heaven .These are the angels that are being mentioned in the verse above

ANGELS

Hebrews 1:14.

They are ministering spirits who live in heaven and are in heaven with God as we speak. They only visit the earth when God commands them to visit or gives them an assignment for a certain individual, family, nation. We have a quite a number of angels that came to earth with a divine purpose and a message for God's people in the bible.

The word angel derives from the Greek word angelos which means a messenger. I will mention a few. In the book of Judges chapter 13 God sent an angel to Manoah and his wife with great news. This couple had no children and the wife was barren for a long time. They had completely accepted the fact that she could not have children but God had other plans.

ANGELS

One day he sent his angel to Manoah's wife when she was working in the fields. He appeared to her and told her God's message and also what He had in store for them as a family and also for the nation Israel.

The great angel even gave her specific instructions on what she should eat during her pregnancy and also the prophetic reason of the child and his upbringing .

Manoah's wife was overjoyed and went home to tell her husband the amazing news. Then Manoah prayed to God that he may also meet the angel of the Lord and hear God's message personally. And faithfully God answered his prayers and the angel reappeared to them and spoke to Manoah.

Angels from God only carry God's word and divine purpose whenever you see an angel ,know that you are on God's mind and heaven is on your case!

The angel of the Lord who appeared to this couple had one agenda on both times he appeared to them , which was to give God's message. After he finished he disappeared ,He did not stick around to help Manoah's wife with her farming or ask to go have some tea or lunch at their house.

He stuck to his assignment and when he was done ,He left! Before I started writing this book ,I had the privilege to talk to a few of God's holy angels and they were revealing to me some of the hidden secrets about Angels that I am going to share with you in this book.

One of the angels I met ,told me that the angels in heaven do not have emotions .They can't feel pain or have feelings or a will and this enables them to fulfill their tasks faithfully .

This is also why the bible mentions that the twenty four elders and angels in heaven constantly worship in heaven .This is was going to be impossible, if they had feelings or emotions ,they would be feeling tired or maybe if they had a bad day ,they would not give God ,the holy and proper worship He deserves .Heaven would become like earth ,inconsistent!

This wasn't always the case though ,God told me that He had to make a swift change because of the terrible situation that happened with the devil,lucifer.The angels could feel ,think and interact ,that's when the devil became jealous of God and convinced a third of the heaven's angels at that time to turn against God.

Isaiah 14 :12 -15

"How you are fallen from heaven,

    O shining star, son of the morning!

You have been thrown down to the earth,

    you who destroyed the nations of the world.

13 For you said to yourself,

    'I will ascend to heaven and set my throne above God's stars.

I will preside on the mountain of the gods

    far away in the north.[e]

14 I will climb to the highest heavens

    and be like the Most High.'

15 Instead, you will be brought down to the place of the dead,

    down to its lowest depths.

ANGELS

Luke 10 :17-18

17 When the seventy-two disciples returned, they joyfully reported to him, "Lord, even the demons obey us when we use your name!"

18 "Yes," he told them, "I saw Satan fall from heaven like lightning! 19 Look, I have given you authority over all the power of the enemy, and you can walk among snakes and scorpions and crush them. Nothing will injure you. 20 But don't rejoice because evil spirits obey you; rejoice because your names are registered in heaven."

Revelation 12 : 7 -17

ANGELS

7 Then there was war in heaven. Michael and his angels fought against the dragon and his angels. 8 And the dragon lost the battle, and he and his angels were forced out of heaven. 9 This great dragon—the ancient serpent called the devil, or Satan, the one deceiving the whole world—was thrown down to the earth with all his angels.

10 Then I heard a loud voice shouting across the heavens,

"It has come at last—
   salvation and power
and the Kingdom of our God,
   and the authority of his Christ.[a]
For the accuser of our brothers and sisters[b]
   has been thrown down to earth—
the one who accuses them
   before our God day and night.

11 And they have defeated him by the blood of the Lamb

   and by their testimony.

And they did not love their lives so much

   that they were afraid to die.

12 Therefore, rejoice, O heavens!

   And you who live in the heavens, rejoice!

But terror will come on the earth and the sea,

   for the devil has come down to you in great anger,

   knowing that he has little time."

13 When the dragon realized that he had been thrown down to the earth, he pursued the woman who had given birth to the male child. 14 But she was given two wings like those of a great eagle so she could fly to the place prepared for her in the wilderness. There she would be cared for and protected from the dragon[c] for a time, times, and half a time.

15 Then the dragon tried to drown the woman with a flood of water that flowed from his mouth. 16 But the earth helped her by opening its mouth and swallowing the river that gushed out from the mouth of the dragon. 17 And the dragon was angry at the woman and declared war against the rest of her children—all who keep God's commandments and maintain their testimony for Jesus.

2 Peter 2 : 4

4 For God did not spare even the angels who sinned. He threw them into hell,[a] in gloomy pits of darkness,[b] where they are being held until the day of judgment.

CHAPTER 4

The Nine Types Of Angels.

There are other type of angels that I am going to go into detail about and reveal in this book. I am also going to reveal in detail about God's angels I got to meet in person and physically like the great angel of war who is second in command after the archangel Michael, one of the cherubim that Prophet Ezekiel in the bible saw in his vision, because of my Spiritual Daddy and Mentor's grace , the great Prophet Moses Brownson.

I will explain and speak more about the heavenly encounters with the God's angels as I continue. God's angels are terrifying creatures! They are not the beautiful angel drawings and baby angels or drawings of cupid that we see. They are very powerful creatures. As I am writting this book the Lord is allowing me to encounter more of them and their presence and their spiritual appearance is overwhelming.

Some of you as you read this book you will feel

ANGELS

God's presence in your room, some you will sense the presence of his holy angels and some of you your spiritual eyes will be open and you will actually see them physically but yet spiritually. These beings show the greatness and great power of God. Heaven is full of these powerful creatures. When you first see them spiritually, I would like to prewarn you don't be terrified!

They are quite scary creatures and you might mistake them for demonic creatures because of how they look. This is why in the bible everytime an angel appeared physically or in a vision to human beings it's first words were "Fear not", because they are terrifying to look at and also God's powerful presence around them is very overwhelming.

I pray that you may have the strength as you experience these holy angelic visitations.

CHAPTER 5

THE SERAPHIM

The first type of angels I will talk about are the Seraphim also known as Seraphs. The name Seraph or Seraphim simply means the "burning one". This Hebrew word describes a type of a celestial or heavenly being. The Seraphim or Seraphs are the angels mentioned in the book of Isaiah 6:1-8.

Prophet Isaiah saw and met these angels in a vision. He describes them as heavenly brings with six wings two wings cover their faces, two cover their feet and the other two they use to fly. They can speak and you can hear them. If you read verse 7 of the book of Isaiah chapter 6 you see that the Prophet Isaiah was interacting with the Seraphim or Seraph in the spiritual realm.

These angels represent God and work for Him. God could have replied the Prophet when he was confessing his sins and feeling unworthy to be seeing what he was seeing. Instead the Seraphim or Seraph flew to him and replied him and also spoke on God's behalf.

Isaiah 6 :1-8

Isaiah's Cleansing and Call

6 It was in the year King Uzziah died[a] that I saw the Lord. He was sitting on a lofty throne, and the train of his robe filled the Temple. 2 Attending him were mighty seraphim, each having six wings. With two wings they covered their faces, with two they covered their feet, and with two they flew. 3 They were calling out to each other,

ANGELS

"Holy, holy, holy is the Lord of Heaven's Armies!

The whole earth is filled with his glory!"

4 Their voices shook the Temple to its foundations, and the entire building was filled with smoke.

5 Then I said, "It's all over! I am doomed, for I am a sinful man. I have filthy lips, and I live among a people with filthy lips. Yet I have seen the King, the Lord of Heaven's Armies."

6 Then one of the seraphim flew to me with a burning coal he had taken from the altar with a pair of tongs. 7 He touched my lips with it and said, "See, this coal has touched your lips. Now your guilt is removed, and your sins are forgiven."

8 Then I heard the Lord asking, "Whom should I send as a messenger to this people? Who will go for us?"

CHAPTER 6

THE CHERUBIM

The second angels I will talk about are the Cherubim. A cherub in the Hebrew language means "mighty one" and I can understand why they were given this name because they are definitely mighty and very powerful! I mentioned that I was going to include my powerful encounters with God's angels. This is one of the angels I have seen and met in person.

The Cherubim are also the same angels Prophet Ezekiel talks about in the book of Ezekiel chapter 10 ,He describes the angels also having six wings and sparkling wheels beside them which have eyes all over ,these wheels sparkle like beryl and are all alike ,they also have a second wheel attached to them that turns crosswise .

These wheels allow them to move in any four directions they face without turning when the move.These wheels are also called the whirling wheels.The Cherubim also have eyes all over their bodies, on their six wings ,on their hands,and on their backs.

Each Cherub has four different faces ,one is a face of an ox, the second a face of a human,the third a face of a lion and the fourth is a face of an eagle.

ANGELS

These angels are very powerful and terrifying to look at. When I saw a cherub in person I quickly understood why every time an angel appears to humans it mentions these words first "Fear not". It is because they are terrifying creatures ,if you are misinformed you will definitely think they are demons or evil spirits.

The word angel sounds simple and beautiful ,when you hear it , you wouldn't expect to see a terrifying heavenly being.

I will explain more about my powerful encounter with the Cherub below when I talk about my other experiences with God's angels.

Ezekiel 10 :1-20

The Lord's Glory Leaves the Temple

10 In my vision I saw what appeared to be a throne of blue lapis lazuli above the crystal surface over the heads of the cherubim. 2 Then the Lord spoke to the man in linen clothing and said, "Go between the whirling wheels beneath the cherubim, and take a handful of burning coals and scatter them over the city." He did this as I watched. 3 The cherubim were standing at the south end of the Temple when the man went in, and the cloud of glory filled the inner courtyard. 4 Then the glory of the Lord rose up from above the cherubim and went over to the entrance of the Temple. The Temple was filled with this cloud of glory, and the courtyard glowed brightly with the glory of the Lord. 5 The moving wings of the cherubim sounded like the voice of God Almighty[a] and could be heard even in the outer courtyard.

6 The Lord said to the man in linen clothing, "Go between the cherubim and take some burning coals from between the wheels." So the man went in and stood beside one of the wheels. 7 Then one of the cherubim reached out his hand and took some live coals from the fire burning among them. He put the coals into the hands of the man in linen clothing, and the man took them and went out. 8 (All the cherubim had what looked like human hands under their wings.)

9 I looked, and each of the four cherubim had a wheel beside him, and the wheels sparkled like beryl. 10 All four wheels looked alike and were made the same; each wheel had a second wheel turning crosswise within it. 11 The cherubim could move in any of the four directions they faced, without turning as they moved. They went straight in the direction they faced, never turning aside. 12 Both the cherubim and the wheels were covered with eyes. The cherubim had eyes all over their

bodies, including their hands, their backs, and their wings. 13 I heard someone refer to the wheels as "the whirling wheels." 14 Each of the four cherubim had four faces: the first was the face of an ox,[b] the second was a human face, the third was the face of a lion, and the fourth was the face of an eagle.

15 Then the cherubim rose upward. These were the same living beings I had seen beside the Kebar River. 16 When the cherubim moved, the wheels moved with them. When they lifted their wings to fly, the wheels stayed beside them. 17 When the cherubim stopped, the wheels stopped. When they flew upward, the wheels rose up, for the spirit of the living beings was in the wheels.

18 Then the glory of the Lord moved out from the entrance of the Temple and hovered above the cherubim. 19 And as I watched, the cherubim flew with their wheels to the east gate of the Lord's Temple. And the glory of the God of Israel hovered

above them.

20 These were the same living beings I had seen beneath the God of Israel when I was by the Kebar River. I knew they were cherubim, 21 for each had four faces and four wings and what looked like human hands under their wings. 22 And their faces were just like the faces of the beings I had seen at the Kebar, and they traveled straight ahead, just as the others had.

The Cherub is also the angel God sent to guard and protect the garden of Eden after Adam and Eve were driven out.

Genesis 3:24

24 After sending them out, the Lord God stationed

ANGELS

mighty cherubim to the east of the Garden of Eden. And he placed a flaming sword that flashed back and forth to guard the way to the tree of life.

Lastly ,on the Cherubim ,the devil before he became the devil he was one of the Cherubim.He was a mighty guardian angel with so much beauty and splendor ,who guarded the garden of Eden.His robes were made of expensive precious stones.He was full of wisdom and a sight of perfection until pride and evil filled his heart.

He became so haughty and full of himself , extremely admiring himself and what God had given him to the point that he became delusional and started to think that he was better than God and could take over him .This was the biggest mistake and our greatest lesson about pride we could learn. Pride is demeaning and dangerous, when you become proud, God will humble you and you will fall.

Ezekiel 28:12-19

"You were the model of perfection,

    full of wisdom and exquisite in beauty.

13 You were in Eden,

    the garden of God.

Your clothing was adorned with every precious stone[b]—

    red carnelian, pale-green peridot, white moonstone,

    blue-green beryl, onyx, green jasper,

    blue lapis lazuli, turquoise, and emerald—

all beautifully crafted for you

    and set in the finest gold.

They were given to you

ANGELS

    on the day you were created.
14 I ordained and anointed you
    as the mighty angelic guardian.[c]
You had access to the holy mountain of God
    and walked among the stones of fire.

15 "You were blameless in all you did
    from the day you were created
    until the day evil was found in you.
16 Your rich commerce led you to violence,
    and you sinned.
So I banished you in disgrace
    from the mountain of God.
I expelled you, O mighty guardian,
    from your place among the stones of fire.
17 Your heart was filled with pride
    because of all your beauty.

Your wisdom was corrupted

   by your love of splendor.

So I threw you to the ground

   and exposed you to the curious gaze of kings.

18 You defiled your sanctuaries

   with your many sins and your dishonest trade.

So I brought fire out from within you,

   and it consumed you.

I reduced you to ashes on the ground

   in the sight of all who were watching.

19 All who knew you are appalled at your fate.

   You have come to a terrible end,

   and you will exist no more."

face, and with two he covered his feet, and with two he flew.

Exodus 25:20

"The cherubim shall have their wings spread upward, covering the mercy seat with their wings and facing one another; the faces of the cherubim are to be turned toward the mercy seat.

Ezekiel 1:6

Each of them had four faces and four wings.

Ezekiel 10:5

Moreover, the sound of the wings of the cherubim was heard as far as the outer court, like the voice of

God Almighty when He speaks.

Ezekiel 10:12

Their whole body, their backs, their hands, their wings and the wheels were full of eyes all around, the wheels belonging to all four of them.

Exodus 25:18

"You shall make two cherubim of gold, make them of hammered work at the two ends of the mercy seat.

Hebrews 9:5

and above it were the cherubim of glory overshadowing the mercy seat; but of these things we cannot now speak in detail.

Ezekiel 10:15

Then the cherubim rose up. They are the living beings that I saw by the river Chebar.

Ezekiel 10:8

The cherubim appeared to have the form of a man's hand under their wings.

Ezekiel 10:18

Then the glory of the LORD departed from the threshold of the temple and stood over the cherubim.

Exodus 25:19

"Make one cherub at one end and one cherub at the other end; you shall make the cherubim of one piece with the mercy seat at its two ends.

1 Kings 8:7

For the cherubim spread their wings over the place of the ark, and the cherubim made a covering over the ark and its poles from above.

Exodus 25:22

Verse Concepts

"There I will meet with you; and from above the mercy seat, from between the two cherubim which are upon the ark of the testimony, I will speak to you about all that I will give you in commandment for the sons of Israel.

Isaiah 6:3

Verse Concepts

And one called out to another and said, "Holy, Holy, Holy, is the LORD of hosts, The whole earth is full of His glory."

2 Chronicles 3:11

Verse Concepts

The wingspan of the cherubim was twenty cubits; the wing of one, of five cubits, touched the wall of the house, and its other wing, of five cubits, touched the wing of the other cherub.

Ezekiel 10:2

And He spoke to the man clothed in linen and said, "Enter between the whirling wheels under the cherubim and fill your hands with coals of fire from between the cherubim and scatter them over the city." And he entered in my sight.

Ezekiel 10:16

Now when the cherubim moved, the wheels would go beside them; also when the cherubim lifted up their wings to rise from the ground, the wheels would not turn from beside them.

Ezekiel 11:22

Then the cherubim lifted up their wings with the wheels beside them, and the glory of the God of Israel hovered over them.

Exodus 37:9

ANGELS

The cherubim had their wings spread upward, covering the mercy seat with their wings, with their faces toward each other; the faces of the cherubim were toward the mercy seat.

Ezekiel 9:3

Then the glory of the God of Israel went up from the cherub on which it had been, to the threshold of the temple. And He called to the man clothed in linen at whose loins was the writing case.

Ezekiel 10:4

Then the glory of the LORD went up from the cherub to the threshold of the temple, and the temple was filled with the cloud and the court was filled with the brightness of the glory of the LORD.

Revelation 4:8

And the four living creatures, each one of them having six wings, are full of eyes around and within; and day and night they do not cease to say, "HOLY, HOLY, HOLY is THE LORD GOD, THE ALMIGHTY, WHO WAS AND WHO IS AND WHO IS TO COME."

ANGELS

Exodus 26:31

"You shall make a veil of blue and purple and scarlet material and fine twisted linen; it shall be made with cherubim, the work of a skillful workman.

Psalm 80:1

Oh, give ear, Shepherd of Israel, You who lead Joseph like a flock; You who are enthroned above the cherubim, shine forth!

Isaiah 37:16

ANGELS

"O LORD of hosts, the God of Israel, who is enthroned above the cherubim, You are the God, You alone, of all the kingdoms of the earth You have made heaven and earth.

Psalm 8:7-10

In my distress I called to the Lord;
   I cried to my God for help.
From his temple he heard my voice;
   my cry came before him, into his ears.
7 The earth trembled and quaked,
   and the foundations of the mountains shook;

they trembled because he was angry.

8 Smoke rose from his nostrils;

consuming fire came from his mouth,

burning coals blazed out of it.

9 He parted the heavens and came down;

dark clouds were under his feet.

10 He mounted the cherubim and flew;

he soared on the wings of the wind.

CHAPTER 7

THE THRONES OR OPHANIMS

The third angels are called Thrones or Ophanims ,these powerful angels are the carrier's of God's throne .Hence their name Thrones.They are also always around God's throne.Prophet Daniel had a vision of the Thrones,He saw them around God's throne serving Him in Daniel 7:9-14.

They are also called Ophanim which mean wheels or Galgallin.Thrones are sometimes equated with Ophanim (Wheels or Galgallin), since the throne of God is usually depicted as being moved by wheels as in the vision of Prophet Daniel in the same book of Daniel 7:9 -14

Daniel 7:9-14

9 I watched as thrones were put in place

   and the Ancient One[a] sat down to judge.

His clothing was as white as snow,

   his hair like purest wool.

He sat on a fiery throne

   with wheels of blazing fire,

10 and a river of fire was pouring out,

   flowing from his presence.

Millions of angels ministered to him;

   many millions stood to attend him.

Then the court began its session,

   and the books were opened.

The Lord also personally revealed to me that they are powerful and they can sing .They sing around His throne in Heaven day and night.One of their main tasks in Heaven is to please God with their voices.They are a sweet melody in his ears when they sing praises to Him.

The Thrones are called to worship and to assist the other holy angels I mentioned above in serving God around His throne.Whenever you see a Throne ,you know God is present .

The 4th Angels group are the Dominions or Lordships.

The word "Dominions" derives from the latin word called dominatio meaning the exercise of control or influence over someone or something, or the state of being so controlled.

In the Greek language it is translated as kyriotetes. "Lordships" or "Dominions" are presented as the hierarchy of celestial beings "Lordships" in some English translations of the De Coelesti Hierarchia. The Dominions regulate the duties of lower angels. It is only with extreme rarity that the angelic lords make themselves physically known to humans.

The Dominions look like divinely beautiful humans with a pair of feathered wings, much like the common representation of angels, but they may be distinguished from other groups by wielding orbs of light fastened to the heads of their scepters or on the pommel of their swords.

Ephesians 1:21

21 far above all rule and authority and power and dominion [whether angelic or human], and [far above] every name that is named [above every title that can be conferred], not only in this age and world but also in the one to come.

Colossians 1:16

16 For [a]by Him all things were created in heaven and on earth, [things] visible and invisible, whether thrones or dominions or rulers or authorities; all things were created and exist through Him [that is, by His activity] and for Him.

CHAPTER 8

THE VIRTUES OR STRONGHOLDS

The 5th angels group are called Virtues or Strongholds. These angels are those through which signs and miracles are made in the world. The term appears to be linked to the attribute "might", from the Greek root dynamis found in the book of Ephesians 1:21, which is also translated as "Virtue" or "Power"

From Pseudo-Dionysius the Areopagite's De Coelesti Hierarchia:"The name of the holy Virtues signifies a certain powerful and unshakable virility welling forth into all their Godlike energies; not being weak and feeble for any reception of the divine Illuminations granted to it; mounting upwards in fullness of power to an assimilation with God; never falling away from the divine life through its own weakness, but ascending unwaveringly to the superessential virtue which is the source of virtue: fashioning itself, as far as it may, in virtue; perfectly turned towards the source of virtue, and flowing forth providentially to those below it, abundantly filling them with virtue."

THE POWERS AND AUTHORITIES

The 6th category of angels are called Powers or Authorities The "Powers" or "Authorities", this word translated in Greek is called exousiai.These are the holy angels mentioned in the book of Ephesians 3 :10 .The primary duty of the "Powers" is to supervise the movements of the heavenly bodies in order to ensure that the cosmos remains in order.Being warrior angels, they also oppose evil spirits, especially those that make use of the matter in the universe, and often cast evil spirits to detention places. These angels are usually represented as soldiers wearing full armor and helmet, and also having defensive and offensive weapons such as shields and spears or chains respectively.

Ephesians 3:10

10 So now through the church the multifaceted wisdom of God [in all its countless aspects] might now be made known [revealing the mystery] to the [angelic] rulers and authorities in the heavenly places.

Revelation 10

The Angel and the Little Book

10 Then I saw another mighty angel coming down from heaven, clothed in a cloud, with a rainbow (halo) over his head; and his face was like the sun, and his feet (legs) were like columns of fire; 2 and he had a little book (scroll) open in his hand. He set his right foot on the sea and his left foot on the land; 3 and he shouted with a loud voice, like the roaring of a lion [compelling attention and inspiring awe]; and when he had shouted out, the seven peals of

thunder spoke with their own voices [uttering their message in distinct words]. 4 And when the seven peals of thunder had spoken, I was about to write; but I heard a voice from heaven saying, "Seal up the things which the seven peals of thunder have spoken and do not write them down." 5 Then the angel whom I had seen standing on the sea and the land raised his right hand [to swear an oath] to heaven, 6 and swore [an oath] by [the name of] Him who lives forever and ever, who created heaven and the things in it, and the earth and the things in it, and the sea and the things in it, that there will be delay no longer, 7 but [a]when it is time for the [b]trumpet call of the seventh angel, when he is about to sound, then the mystery of God [that is, His hidden purpose and plan] is finished, as He announced the gospel to His servants the prophets.

8 Then the voice which I heard from heaven, I heard again speaking to me, and saying, "Go, take the book (scroll) which is open in the hand of the angel who is standing on the sea and on the land." 9 So I

went up to the angel and told him to give me the little book. And he said to me, "Take it and eat it; it will make your stomach bitter, but in your mouth it will be as sweet as honey." 10 So I took the little book from the angel's hand and ate it, and in my mouth it was as sweet as honey; but once I had swallowed it, my stomach was [c]bitter. 11 Then they said to me, "You must prophesy again concerning many peoples and nations and languages and kings."

Revelation 11 Amplified Bible

The Two Witnesses

11 Then there was given to me a [a]measuring rod like a staff; and someone said, "[b]Rise and measure the temple of God and the altar [of incense], and [count] those who worship in it. 2 But leave out the court [of the Gentiles] which is outside the temple and do not measure it, because it has

been given to the Gentiles (the nations); and they will trample the holy city for forty-two months (three and one-half years). 3 And I will grant authority to My two witnesses, and they will prophesy for twelve hundred and sixty days (forty-two months; three and one-half years), dressed in [c]sackcloth." 4 These [witnesses] are the two olive trees and the two lampstands which stand before the Lord of the earth. 5 And if anyone wants to harm them, fire comes out of their mouth and devours their enemies; so if anyone wants to harm them, he must be killed in this way. 6 These [two witnesses] have the power [from God] to shut up the sky, so that no rain will fall during the days of their prophesying [regarding judgment and salvation]; and they have power over the waters (seas, rivers) to turn them into blood, and to strike the earth with every [kind of] plague, as often as they wish.

7 When they have finished their testimony and given their evidence, the beast that comes up out of the abyss (bottomless pit) will wage war with them,

and overcome them and kill them. 8 And their dead bodies will lie exposed in the open street of the great city (Jerusalem), which in a spiritual sense is called [by the symbolic and allegorical names of] Sodom and Egypt, where also their Lord was crucified. 9 Those from the peoples and tribes and languages and nations [d]look at their dead bodies for three and a half days, and will not allow their dead bodies to be laid in a tomb. 10 And those [non-believers] who live on the earth will gloat over them and rejoice; and they will send gifts [in celebration] to one another, because these two prophets tormented and troubled those who live on the earth.

11 But after three and a half days, the breath of life from God came into them, and they stood on their feet; and great fear and panic fell on those who were watching them. 12 And the two witnesses heard a loud voice from heaven saying to them,

"Come up here." Then they ascended into heaven in the cloud, and their enemies watched them. 13 And in that [very] hour there was a great earthquake, and a tenth of the city fell and was destroyed; seven thousand [e]people were killed in the earthquake, and the rest [who survived] were overcome with terror, and [f]they glorified the God of heaven [as they recognized His awesome power].

14 The second woe is past; behold, the third woe is coming quickly.

The Seventh Trumpet—Christ's Reign Foreseen

15 Then the seventh angel sounded [his trumpet]; and there were loud voices in heaven, saying,

"The kingdom (dominion, rule) of the world has become the kingdom of our Lord and of His Christ; and He will reign forever and ever." 16 And the twenty-four elders, who sit on their thrones before

God, fell face downward and worshiped God, 17 saying,

"To You we give thanks, O Lord God Almighty [the Omnipotent, the Ruler of all], Who are and Who were, because You have taken Your great power and the sovereignty [which is rightly Yours] and have [now] begun to reign. 18 And the nations (Gentiles) became enraged, and Your wrath and indignation came, and the time came for the dead to be judged, and [the time came] to reward Your bond-servants the prophets and the saints (God's people) and those who fear Your name, the small and the great, and [the time came] to destroy the destroyers of the earth."

19 And the temple of God which is in heaven was opened; and the ark of His covenant appeared in His temple, and there were flashes of lightning, loud rumblings and peals of thunder and an earthquake and a great hailstorm.

CHAPTER 9

THE PRINCIPALITIES OR RULERS.

The 7th Category of angels are the Principalities or Rulers. The word "Principalities" derives from the latin word principatus also translated as "Princedoms" and "Rulers", in the Greek language. The Principalities or Rulers are the angels that guide and protect nations, or groups of peoples, and institutions such as the Church. The Principalities preside over the bands of angels and charge them with fulfilling the divine ministry. There are some who administer and some who assist.

Their duty also is to carry out the orders given to them by the upper sphere angels and bequeath blessings to the physical world. Their task is to oversee groups of people. They are the educators and guardians of the realm of earth. Like beings related to the world of the germinal ideas, they were designed to inspire living things to many things such as art or science.

Paul used the term rule and authority in Ephesians 1:21, and rulers and authorities in Ephesians 3:10.

Ephesians 3:10

10 So now through the church the multifaceted wisdom of God [in all its countless aspects] might now be made known [revealing the mystery] to the [angelic] rulers and authorities in the heavenly places.

THE ARCHANGELS.

The 8th group of angels are the Archangels.

The word "archangel" comes from the Greek word ἀρχάγγελος (archangelos), meaning chief angel, a translation of the Hebrew רַאְלָמ־בַר (rav-mal'ákh). It derives from the Greek archein, meaning to be first in rank or power, and angelos which means messenger or envoy. The word is only used twice in the New Testament: 1 Thessalonians 4:16 and Jude 1:9. Only the Archangel Michael is mentioned by name in the New Testament.

1 Thessalonians 4:16

16 For the Lord Himself will come down from heaven with a shout of command, with the voice of the [a]archangel and with the [blast of the] trumpet of God, and the dead in Christ will rise first.

Jude 1:9

But when [even] the archangel Michael, contending with the devil, judicially argued (disputed) about the body of Moses, he dared not [presume to] bring an abusive condemnation against him, but [simply] said, The Lord rebuke you!

Gabriel is also an archangel. This the arch angel who visited Mary and Joseph announcing the birth of our Lord Jesus Christ this is mentioned in Luke 1:26-38. He also appeared to Prophet Daniel in a vision with a reply to his prayer and fasting in the book Daniel 9:21-23. He also visited Zechariah with good news of his wife's miracle pregnancy in Luke 1:8-17.

Luke 1:8-17

Birth of John the Baptist Foretold

5 In the days of Herod [the Great], king of Judea, there was a certain priest whose name was [c]Zacharias, of [d]the division of Abijah. His wife was [e]a descendant of Aaron [the first high priest of Israel], and her name was Elizabeth. 6 They both were righteous (approved) in the sight of God, walking blamelessly in all the commandments and requirements of the Lord. 7 But they were childless, because Elizabeth was barren, and they were both far advanced in years.

8 Now it happened while Zacharias was serving as priest before God in the appointed order of his priestly division, 9 as was the custom of the priesthood, he was chosen by lot to enter [the sanctuary of] the temple of the Lord and [f]burn incense [on the altar of incense]. 10 And all the congregation was praying outside [in the court of

the temple] at the hour of the incense offering. 11 And an angel of the Lord appeared to him, standing to the right of the altar of incense. 12 When Zacharias saw the angel, he was troubled and overcome with fear. 13 But the angel said to him, "Do not be afraid, Zacharias, because your petition [in prayer] was heard, and your wife Elizabeth will bear you a son, and you will name him [g]John. 14 You will have great joy and delight, and many will rejoice over his birth, 15 for he will be great and distinguished in the sight of the Lord; and will never drink wine or liquor, and he will be filled with and empowered to act by the Holy Spirit while still in his mother's womb. 16 He will turn many of the sons of Israel back [from sin] to [love and serve] the Lord their God. 17 It is he who will go as a forerunner before Him in the spirit and power of Elijah, to turn the hearts of the fathers back to the children, and the disobedient to the attitude of the righteous [which is to seek and submit to the will of God]—in order to make ready a people [perfectly] prepared [spiritually and morally] for the Lord."

18 And Zacharias said to the angel, "How will I be certain of this? For I am an old man and my wife is advanced in age." 19 The angel replied and said to him, "I am Gabriel; I stand and minister in the [very] presence of God, and I have been sent [by Him] to speak to you and to bring you this good news. 20 [h]Listen carefully, you will be continually silent and unable to speak until the day when these things take place, because you did not believe what I told you; but my words will be fulfilled at their proper time."

21 The people [outside in the court] were waiting for Zacharias, and were wondering about his long delay in the temple. 22 But when he did come out, he was unable to speak to them. They realized that he had seen a vision in the temple; and he kept making signs to them, and remained mute. 23 When his time of priestly service was finished, he returned to his home.

ANGELS

24 Now after this his wife Elizabeth became pregnant, and for five months she secluded herself completely, saying, 25 "This is how the Lord has dealt with me in the days when He looked with favor on me, to take away my [i]disgrace among men."

The other Archangel is Raphael. His name of appears only in the Book of Tobit (Tobias). Tobit is considered Deuterocanonical by Roman Catholics (both Eastern and Western Rites), Eastern Orthodox Christians, and Anglicans. Tobit had an angelic visitation from Raphael and he wrote about him in his book, The Book of Tobit. Raphael said to Tobias that he was "one of the seven who stand before the Lord", and it is generally believed that Michael and Gabriel are two of the other six.

The fourth archangel is Uriel whose name literally means "Light of God." Uriel's name is found in the second Book of Esdras (fourth Books of Esdras in the Latin Vulgate). In the book, he unveils seven prophecies to the prophet Ezra, after whom the book is named. He also plays a role in the apocryphal Book of Enoch.

I also had the privilege of meeting Uriel in a vision of the night, I was in a spiritual warfare with a marine spirit who lives in the water and as I was killing it ,Uriel came to help me .His name Uriel ,"light of God "describes his appearance as well his body frame is made out of the light of God and he shines like a led light pipe.

The seven archangels are also the seven spirits of God that stand before the throne described in the Book of Enoch, and in the Book of Revelation.

The Seven Archangels are the guardian angels of nations and countries, and are concerned with the issues and events surrounding these, including politics, military matters, commerce and trade etc.

CHAPTER 10

ANGELS

MY SUPERNATURAL ANGELIC VISITATIONS.

I mentioned above that God had instructed me to share about my personal and prophetic encounters with the powerful angels. The spiritual world is very real and very accessible but in order to participate in it you have to be introduced, birthed or ushered into it.

There are also levels you have to go through in the prophetic, before I met my Spiritual Father, the Great Prophet Moses Brownson, I moved and functioned in a lower level, this level of vision in the prophetic is called hazon in Hebrew. This word means vision. In this prophetic level you can dream of angels, see angels spiritually, discern their presence.

My first encounter was in 2007 ,and I was 17 years old .An angel appeared in my room and he whispered in my right ear.I will never forget his words .At that time I was still in the world and was a little bit on the wild side

.I knew that God existed but didn't pay too much attention about what he wanted or expected of me.I was young and at that time I did a lot of partying.I hung around the wrong group of friends and because , I didn't have a close relationship with God ,I didn't know that partying and clubbing was a bad thing .

ANGELS

I had seen every one in my family living this kind of lifestyle as soon as they were adults or old enough ,and also my friends back then and everyone else that was around me lived and behaved this way.

My mom was not proud of it because she wanted to protect me from rapists and terrible incidences as a teenager but I considered myself an adult and I always assured her that I would becareful every time I went out.

So at that time my friends and I were absolutely crazy .Every weekend either on a Friday or a Saturday was a party night or club night.I didn't enjoy it as much as they did ,but I kept on doing it because I didn't know any better and I had accepted that this is how my life was going to be as a young "adult".

ANGELS

We would go out have a few drinks and dance all night .I was a single young lady and for some reason ,I thought was going to find a cute and handsome boyfriend every time ,I would go out.That dream never came true ,I couldn't stand the men that approached me at these parties so ,I quickly gave that up.

The wild lifestyle of parties went on for an entire year and I wanted it to stop but I didn't know how. Everyone I knew was living this way.Up until that glorious afternoon when God sent an angel into my room .He whispered gently over my right shoulder and into my right ear and said "Do you think you are going to go to heaven or hell with the way you are living?"

I was shocked and troubled because I had just heard a clear voice whispering in my ear asking me this question.Ever since that day I decided to change my life and found out more about God and what he expected of me.

My second encounter with an angel in the hazon level was in the year of 2009 and I was 19 years old. I had a vision of the night, in my dream I was sleeping on top of a bunk bed, then all of a sudden there was a big and tall heavenly being standing next to me shinning brightly, in a white robe. When I noticed him, He began to speak and this is what he said "You want to see an angel?, you want to see an angel?" As he was speaking the entire room including the bunk bed began to vigorously shake as if there was an earthquake taking place.

The shaking kept on increasing as I became more aware in my dream that he was the angel and he was directly talking to me. My night vision stopped there and I woke up.

ANGELS

When I woke up I realized that God had answered my prayer ,because I had personally embarked on a three month fast for spiritual growth as a young prophet and I wanted to know more about God's angels and God's kingdom.

My 3rd encounter was in the same year of 2009 at 19 years old ,I was at my bus top waiting for a bus ,and all of a sudden an angel appeared in human form he was holding a wheel ,He asked me if I knew what time the bus was coming and I politely answered back that I didn't know , and advised him to call the bus line and find out ,the automated service always announced the hourly bus schedule.

ANGELS

When I told him this ,he then changed the subject and started talking about God and gave me a prophetic message . When he finished delivering his message our bus came ,but instead of taking the bus he left the bus stop and walked away .I was in awe and shocked because the message was so powerful and I couldn't believe what had just physically happened before my eyes in that bus stop.

My 4th encounter was in 2010 and I was 20 years old .I was listening to a powerful teaching on angels and visions on YouTube by the great Prophet Uebert Angel ,the teaching was very powerful and I was extremely stirred up in my spirit.I started to cry out to God so that I could see an angel! As I was praying all of a sudden the angel appeared and he was sitting on my bed ,I was terrified! There was an unknown big creature on my bed and he had a strong, overwhelming presence!That was my first open vision and the beginning of many.He didn't say a word but he was just looking at me ,giving me that here I am kind of a look ,God has answered your prayer prophet.

I was so scared I prayed to God again and asked him to ask the angel to leave because it was too much for me,and God answered my prayer and the angel disappeared.

My 5th encounter happened when I met my Spiritual Daddy ,As a prophet ,my Daddy prayed for me ,anointed me ,unlocked me and ushered me into his dimension.In 2018 at the age of 27 ,I began to see angels physically and experience them at a greater level.

When I was released into the prophetic office my

eyes were open and I began to operate in the Mara level. The word mara is a Hebrew word which means vision, mirror and mode of revelation. In this level the angels and the spiritual world manifest physically. In the hazon level when you see an angel it is a spiritual, faint image when it's an open vision, the angel is in a spiritual form and you can walk through the angel. In the mara level you can't walk through the angel, the angel is physical, if you try to walk through the angel, you will fall because you will actually bump into the angel. The angel's body feels like any other physical object.

Under my Daddy's anointing and grace I have had the privilege to meet the most mighty and high ranking angels. I got to meet the arch angel Gabriel he has appeared to me physically several times with a message from God, walked with me in the streets, keeping me company and assuring me that God is with me in the city and country he sent me to prophesy and preach the gospel.

ANGELS

I also had the chance to meet the incredible and kind angel of war ,I won't mention his name but he is the angel that is second in command of the arch angel Michael.The first time I met him ,He appeared in my room and stood at a corner ,I was about to fall asleep and when I saw him there,I froze in my bed because he is a powerful creature and his figure was terrifying ,He didn't move or say word to me but was just looking at me .I quickly asked God who he was and He explained and assured me all was well and He told me who he was.We have become best of friends now ,He accompanies me everywhere I go most of the time and he helps me a lot in spiritual warfare.

The other encounter also happened in my room , as I was writting this book I Cherub appeared.God sent one Cherub to visit me, because they are so powerful , in that moment ,I felt like Prophet

Ezekiel in the bible .I felt like I was reliving how he felt in his vision with the Cherubim. The Cherub was very lively ,he was moving around my room and he showed me all of his four different faces.It was quite an experience because he is so loving and wanted me to see how he looks like, from his wings full of eyes all over and his body and whirling wheels also full of eyes but it was so petrifying.

These angels are very powerful creatures .As I was in the room I constantly begged God to ask him to kindly leave but the Cherub kept on getting closer and closer so that I could really see him and would be able to explain to you how he looks like .At one point I closed my eyes but as a prophet I could still see and feel him spiritually .God's angels are very mighty creatures!

The other experiences I had were cute ,like the

ANGELS

time I was watching a live broadcast of my Spiritual Daddy on Facebook a beautiful angel ,who looks like a white horse appeared in my living room and nudged me with his head to say hello. I almost fell when he greeted me ,it was very adorable .The other time God came in my house with angel who is a lion with wings ,he was so cute ,he wanted me to pat him on his head to greet him and I did it. After the patting on his head ,he sat down on my carpeted floor whilst I continued in prayer, speaking to God.

My life has tremendously changed and evolved in the Mara level ,angels have become a part of my every day life .They are always with me ,when I am sad ,happy, angry etc. One time I was very sad about something and I began to cry, and an angel came and offered me a tissue in the spirit .How sweet is that ! Sometimes they tickle me so that I have joy or ,constantly give me high fives , big ups or hugs ,they are very powerful but sweet and kind .My life would be so lonely without them because as a prophet ,your life is very spiritual and very different from everyone else ,you see ,hear and experience what they can't on a daily basis.So with God's angels , I am never alone ,they keep me company and are great friends of mine!

CHAPTER 11

THE END TIME ANGELS.

Lastly but not least when God told me to write this book ,He began to tell me more of the hidden mysteries in the world .He revealed to me that there is also another breed of angels who exist on earth .This is not demonic but it was a part of God's plan as well.He just didn't publicly disclose it,but as we are living in the end times ,the time is coming when this truth will be revealed.

These angels are born of women like regular human babies.They are human but they also have angelic D.N.A. God told me that many of them are clueless that they are angels ,however spiritually and physically they go through what other real humans do not go through. Their spirituality is over the top ,meaning they are extremely spiritual. God also told me that these angels are 80% angelic and 20% human.

In the physical realm ,they look like humans and even live their every day lives like a normal human being. They go to school,work ,drive ,eat, get married,and have children ,etc just like any normal human being.

God created this kind of breed ,to help him in the earth realm. Once God reveals to these angels them,their true identity ,they start to help him build his kingdom and to destroy the devil and his kingdom.

ANGELS

They are like God's secret agents on earth! We are living in the endtimes and this is just a small part of the prophecies in the bible being fufilled.

1 Corinthians 2 :9-13

9 but just as it is written [in Scripture],

"Things which the eye has not seen and the ear has not heard,

And which have not entered the heart of man,

All that God has prepared for those who love Him [who hold Him in affectionate reverence, who obey Him, and who gratefully recognize the benefits that He has bestowed]."

10 For God has unveiled them and revealed them to us through the [Holy] Spirit; for the Spirit searches all things [diligently], even [sounding and measuring] the [profound] depths of God [the divine counsels and things far beyond human understanding]. 11 For what person knows the thoughts and motives of a man except the man's spirit within him? So also no one knows the thoughts of God except the Spirit of God. 12 Now we have received, not the spirit of the world, but the [Holy] Spirit who is from God, so that we may know and understand the [wonderful] things freely given to us by God. 13 We also speak of these things, not in words taught or supplied by human wisdom, but in those taught by the Spirit, combining and interpreting spiritual thoughts with spiritual words [for those being guided by the Holy Spirit].

Daniel 2:28

"However, there is a God in heaven who reveals mysteries, and He has made known to King Nebuchadnezzar what will take place in the latter days This was your dream and the visions in your mind while on your bed.

Daniel 2:47

The king answered Daniel and said, "Surely your God is a God of gods and a Lord of kings and a revealer of mysteries, since you have been able to reveal this mystery."

Daniel 2:19

Then the mystery was revealed to Daniel in a night vision. Then Daniel blessed the God of heaven;

Job 12:22

"He reveals mysteries from the darkness And brings the deep darkness into light.

Daniel 2:22

"It is He who reveals the profound and hidden things; He knows what is in the darkness, And the light dwells with Him.

Jeremiah 33:3

'Call to Me and I will answer you, and I will tell you great and mighty things, which you do not know.'

Daniel 7:16

"I approached one of those who were standing by and began asking him the exact meaning of all this

So he told me and made known to me the interpretation of these things

Daniel 2:29

"As for you, O king, while on your bed your thoughts turned to what would take place in the future; and He who reveals mysteries has made known to you what will take place.

Daniel 2:23

"To You, O God of my fathers, I give thanks and praise, For You have given me wisdom and power; Even now You have made known to me what we requested of You, For You have made known to us the king's matter."

Daniel 2:30

"But as for me, this mystery has not been revealed to me for any wisdom residing in me more than in any other living man, but for the purpose of making the interpretation known to the king, and that you may understand the thoughts of your mind.

Ephesians 6:19

and pray on my behalf, that utterance may be given to me in the opening of my mouth, to make known with boldness the mystery of the gospel,

Ephesians 1:9

He made known to us the mystery of His will, according to His kind intention which He purposed in Him

Colossians 1:27

to whom God willed to make known what is the riches of the glory of this mystery among the Gentiles, which is Christ in you, the hope of glory.

Matthew 13:11

Jesus answered them, "To you it has been granted to know the mysteries of the kingdom of heaven, but to them it has not been granted.

Mark 4:11

And He was saying to them, "To you has been given the mystery of the kingdom of God, but those who are outside get everything in parables,

Luke 8:10

And He said, "To you it has been granted to know

the mysteries of the kingdom of God, but to the rest it is in parables, so that SEEING THEY MAY NOT SEE, AND HEARING THEY MAY NOT UNDERSTAND.

Colossians 1:26

that is, the mystery which has been hidden from the past ages and generations, but has now been manifested to His saints,

Ephesians 3:5

which in other generations was not made known to the sons of men, as it has now been revealed to His holy apostles and prophets in the Spirit;

ANGELS

Ephesians 3:3

that by revelation there was made known to me the mystery, as I wrote before in brief.

www.ingramcontent.com/pod-product-compliance
Lightning Source LLC
Chambersburg PA
CBHW021812220426
43662CB00006B/284